Rich Remembering

Carol Armstrong

Cover painting: Margaret Hemphill Lannan

Rich Remembering by Carol Armstrong

Cover painting: Margaret Hemphill Lannen

Design: Barbara Jones

ISBN: 978-0-692-82289-0

1. Poetry

First Edition

Printed at Fort Orange Press, Albany, NY

Books may be purchased by contacting:

Elizabeth L. Armstrong
38 Heatherbloom Dr.
Lewisburg, PA 17837

Rich Remembering

I am content on a fair night
when I find the moon
where I expect it to be
flinging a splash of light
across my king-sized bed
where I now lie alone
after seventy-one years
of sharing it with my husband.

I still, out of old habit,
don't turn on the light when
I get up in the middle of
the night, though it now
would inconvenience no one
and would greatly benefit me.
Is this a part of remembering?
Does it ensure I shall never forget?

I mourn the emptiness
but cherish the remembering.
I do not mind living in this
half world as well as the one
of *shoes and ships and sealing wax*.
Life is to be lived in all its variety —
good, bad, joyful as well as sad
enhanced by rich remembering.

For Phyllis Katz and Deming Holleran
with all my admiration and gratitude

—CAA

I

\

The Week in Review   3

Inept Juggler   5

By Heart   7

Daybreak   8

Three Dances in Slow Time   9

Subtle Sweetness   12

January This Year   13

Christmas Catalogue   14

Absolution of Snow   15

Funeral on Thursday   16

Three a.m.   19

\\

The Week in Review

MONDAY is serious and purposeful
as a child digging a hole, or watching a beetle.
In an earlier, more orderly time
it was proud to be called Laundry Day.

TUESDAY rains—but is as cheerful as
the shambling waitress in the neighborhood
diner where you go for beans and franks,
banter, friendly insult, and the old-shoe
comfort of casual conversation.

WEDNESDAY repents. It's mid-week—
still time to recover lost opportunities,
glasses, thoughts, friends. Eager to
make amends, undo mistakes, retrieve
what may be salvaged of damaged intent.

THURSDAY wonders, ponders, and
watches the clouds tumble and roll out to sea.
Without fanfare, welcomes the reappearance
of sun, as the child the returning mother.

FRIDAY walks with energy and spirit.
Ideas rattle in its head, as it tilts toward
the weekend, which holds the heady possibility
of fishing the shadowed holes of brooks
where rainbows rest shimmering.

SATURDAY is loud with enthusiasm,
determined to disport itself handsomely.
It wears itself out laughing.

SUNDAY, released from the prohibitions
of generations past, may now launder, mow,
mend, sweep, polish and shop for shoes.

—God only rested on the seventh day because
he'd quite finished the job he'd undertaken—

while SUNDAY has a tangle of loose ends to be tied up
before serious MONDAY returns, purposeful as ever.

Inept Juggler

Life has become
utterly cluttered

like Times Square
at rush hour

each aspect of it
mindlessly finding

its singular path
through the barely

controlled chaos
harried by time

of comings and
inevitable goings

with an urgency
that makes no

distinctions between
vital and trivial

clear duty and desire
vying for priority

each with the urgency
of a juggler's knives

bowling pins, eggs
and delicate teacups

precisely tossed and
in desperate need

of being caught
before the gravity

of the situation
causes them to crash

in a hopeless clatter
to the unforgiving floor.

Is time the cause and culprit
or have I forgotten

in my bewilderment
the secret of serenity?

By Heart

Spring has come again,
The earth is like a child that
knows poems by heart.
                    Rilke

From the stored root-memory
the plant repeats its exuberant poem,
a touch of showing off.

The willow sings its weeping song
in pale feathery green.
The crocus recites short, pithy
nursery rhymes in sing-song
yellow, lavender, and white,

and shouting loudly from bright
petal-cupped mouths, the daffodils
announce in ragged chorus:
Spring has come again . . . again . . . again.

Repeat your poems, child-earth.
I offer mute gratitude
at your facility, your
faultless memory,
the exquisite drama of your unfolding.

Daybreak

Morning breaks
out of the shroud
of night. I do not care
whether its return
is the result of the earth
rotating on its axis, or
some other scientific fact.
Sunrise is a daily miracle.

I am overcome by gratitude
for the green world
that waits as eagerly as I
for sunrise each day
to return the woods animals'
bright night eyes
to their furry daytime bodies.

Do not mistake me.
Night is as necessary as day,
with its own uses.
Without the new day offered
each twenty-four hours,
how can we make a new start,
imagine new possibilities,
forgive ourselves,
and begin anew?

Three Dances in Slow Time

I

Pavane

Black ice has not yet
wholly stopped
the tongue
of the brook.

In two places
it sings out roundly
over smooth stones
erupting through
white crust.

The sun sets to
salmon dusk
silently.

Silently the near-round
moon sweeps up.

In their vast pavane
in their cosmic swing
without sound
in windless waste

they are accompanied
by the dark
triple-tongued music
of the brook
not yet silenced
by black ice.

II

Sarabande

Snow like frozen
cloud formations
melts into new
slow shapes.

Spring is a dream
the snow melts into
the drowsing field
loosing
imagination's
Winter.

Huddled together
for dreaming
daffodils reach
their new cold green
toward an
imagined Spring.

III

Minuet

Minuetted into
patterned grove
requiring
a century of
slow dance

to shape sedate
and solartropic bough
with grace
extend a branch

advance
retreat with
the elegance of eons

the trees step
lightly as a
wind-waft seed

the pattern blown
exactingly by chance
minuetted to a grove
in dance.

Subtle Sweetness

There is a subtle sweetness
in the early morning air
of an early Spring day.

Is it imagined like
the other things for
which we yearn?

Is it the fulfillment
of an anticipated
long-awaited thing?

Is it Spring that
makes its coming
finally so sweet?

Shall I feel
betrayed tomorrow
when it snows?

January This Year

This year January
has been ambivalent,
unable to decide
whether it should be
traditionally cold
or unexpectedly warm.

My mother once
asked me why
all my letters began
with a weather report,
to which I replied
that the weather
"set the stage,"
supplied the backdrop
for whatever I intended
to communicate.

Today the sun
on the fresh snow
dazzles the eye.
Today I am
beguiled into
imagining I can
accomplish all
that's required of me—
my spirits nourished
by the unexpected
warmth
in the winter sun.

Christmas Catalogue

Nestled in a cradle of
juniper and cranberry—
dusty-blue berries
and red ones

a pear half,
white sweet flesh
dripping with juice,
so perfect

evocative of the best
of old memories
so right and proper as
a gift for my sister

who shared ripe pears
with me on the same
sun-warmed rock in the
same childhood.

Absolution of Snow

The snow
seeing no longer
the blossoming of Spring
harvesting of Summer
blazing of Fall

 instead now
looks down on
blackened fern, browned leaf
withered stalk
flattened fields of wolf grass
and late hay

is moved
to spill a generosity
of intricately-designed
flurries of forgiveness
over the earth's dying

an absolution accorded
this exhausted and broken land
till in its good time
a new burgeoning returns.

Funeral on Thursday

"The funeral will be held on
Thursday at St. Michael's Church.
Visiting hours from two to four
today and tomorrow."

No hint in the news-flat TV voice
that this was other than
the occasion to recognize and honor
the long and amiable life
of one of the town's gray-haired,

who'd gone to Wakely High,
graduated, if not with honors
at least with the buoyant
ballooning memory of
his team's undefeated season,

gone into his father's
hardware business and
having his father's genial
way with people
attracted not only customers

but Sally Wentworth, by whom
after a suitable time and rumpled courtship
he had three children
two of whom sprouted his reddish hair
and sported his Irish face

all of whom
"borrowed" candy from

the display near the office door
skinny-dipped in Weymouth Pond
after dark, even in the rain

fought in the school yard
were punished

had Sunday dinner with
their grandfather whom they adored
whose zesty humor and colorful language
they tried to emulate
even to the ancestral lilt of it

all of whom
both the two boys and
the girl, in a different way
looked with anticipation
and a sort of breathless eagerness
toward the secret excitements
of adulthood which to them

seemed to revolve around
owning a car, having
loose change, wearing
whatever funky thing they liked
having a beer and sex

perhaps, though less
immediate in prospect,
a mate, offspring
and a backyard full of dogs.

But this uninflected announcement
concerned a lanky 17-year-old

barely becoming a man
pictured with a rally cap
and lopsided grin

killed in a school-yard fight
with a bull-dog-of-a
16-year-old who landed
a lucky—or unlucky punch,

before he'd got much beyond
a passionate preoccupation
with a battered heap,
Red Sox stats and girls.

I shall be there on Thursday
to lament this uncompleted life
with its unborn possibilities
lopped off to the last generation.
Is there a place in heaven where
lost possibilities are stored?

Three a.m.

The tall clock strikes suddenly
leaving three thin cords of sound
strung out across the deepened dark

of my moonless bedroom, black with
night-thoughts and weary words
left over from aging arguments,

the non-degradable debris of lingering loss
that will outlast love and meaningless memory
exposed by the haunted hours of wakefulness

as the litter of the careless summer season,
winter-buried, is exposed again, exhumed
by mid-March snow-melt
along the hurrying highway.

Again the steadfast Grandfather strikes
the hour, measuring my misery.

II

II

Today It Snows   23

Short   24

More and More   25

Independence   26

Waiting   28

5

Today It Snows

Today it snows softly on my sorrow
roundly mounding the sharp edges of grief,
filling the now empty places
where I used to live, content
where there was reason to dust and sweep,
to cook, do laundry and dishes,
where the reason was worthy,
sufficient and gladdening.

In this quiet softening of loss,
I will make new again—
the mapless landscape into which
I hesitantly plan to live,
making tracks of my own in new snow,
learning things never imagined,
proof that I too have passed this way.

Short

I cut my white hair short
not to appear untidy,
the old lady with a
halo of startled hair.

I cut my nails short
for they now are
brittle and break
unaccountably,
shapeless and sharp.

I cut my long skirts short
to adjust to
current trends,
not to be thought
heedless of fashion.

I cut my conversations short.
I do not tell my dreams
or how it used to be
or give too much advice—
at least I make a
brave attempt—

but sometimes
I would like to
curl up on the bed
pretending to be dead.

More and More

More and more
I am uncertain
on waking
in the morning

whether it's
yesterday, today
or tomorrow.

More and more
the weather
and not circumstance
determines the
day's direction.

Less and less
does the world
need my
direct involvement

and more and more—
by far the most
difficult role
is that of the
grateful recipient

the one who
becomes the ladder
providing the rungs
for others to rise
toward their own
usefulness.

Independence

As the chill wind
whipped by her
graying head,

"Florida is for the
newly-wed or
nearly-dead," she said.

She likes it here
among the
snow-bent trees

where in the
frigid stiff
mid-winter breeze

the ponds
for children's
skating-pleasure freeze.

She loves her
small house on
the mountain road

the woodshed
where her winter
wood is stowed

the August fields
cleared to the walls
she's cleanly mowed.

No Florida for her!

Since losing Seth
she's made her peace
with close and
friendly death

and wants this
crisp clear air to be
her final breath.

Waiting

The gods of our circular year
and four distinct seasons
have this year mislaid Spring.

Whether it got lost in the dark
recesses of a cave where
seasons are stored or

lost in a game of pitch and toss,
none of us knows.

The days have become
infinitesimally longer—
the sun shines on
fields of snow, but they just
glisten, do not melt.

My spirits fail to warm my body,
or my body, my spirits.

Things are not as they should be.
One of the great wheels
of the year has slid
into a ditch, and we who've
paid our tuppence for the ride

sit baffled and confused
unaccustomed to going nowhere
whether for pleasure or dragged,
unwilling, by circumstance.

When will the great hemlock boughs
let go their mounded burden of snow?
Shall I ever be released
from my glistening burden of loss?

III

III

Tree Trunks 33

The Best Poems Come Unbidden 34

Psalm 35

I've Written Foolishly 37

I Want to Read Poems 38

Tree Trunks

Tree trunks whited out
on the north side only

the south side black with
the absence of snow

the south side the only
readable landscape.

The north side invisibly
bearing the balancing burden
of what must be said,

skeletal thought sharing
with visible analogy
the weight of the poem.

The Best Poems Come Unbidden

It is not easy
to clear a place
inside you where
a poem may
come of its
own accord
and breathe—
not bidden
or implored.

But the effort
is rewarded
occasionally
when a poem
invents itself
from thin air

and finds its way
into receiving grace.

Psalm

Honor your poets,
all ye lands,
cherish and hold them
among you
as seers and servants
of the people.

They sacrifice
for you daily
giving their bodies
to be lightning rods
among the nations,
grounding
the god-flung bolts,
shuddering them
transformed
to earth.

They lift their human arms
above your homes,
above your heads
catching the power
Vulcan-forged, and let it run
their bodies through.

You'll see them
sometimes
as human sacrifice,
themselves burnt offering,
a holy destruction
for your sake

their frail humanity
unable to withstand the charge,
their mind the last bright ash
upon the altar stone.

Honor and celebrate
this burnt-out life
consumed for you.

There but for some kind
of grace you go.
There bright-burns
one who's seared by
too much pain,
too much joy,
too much conductivity.

Don't weep for them
nor pity.
Only raise up
monuments of memory
and at your hearth
make fresh-baked bread
and lentil soup, thank-offerings
the smell of which
will reach them
where at long, long last
they rest.

I've Written Foolishly

I've written foolishly of late.
I hate the words strung out
upon the page
in rage against the waste of haste.

But first—and worst—
I cannot stand the grand defeat
of neatly written hand
and shallow thought—all chaff
with no sustaining wheat.

I Want to Read Poems

I want to read poems
till I'm full-up—
till night falls and lights
must be turned on

till the poets I know
have told me the last
truths they've learned
about themselves

in a first language
unique to them
translated for me
into telling gesture.

I am emptied,
a prerequisite
to being filled, and
go gladly with them

to that place of rich detail
and muscle memory
no baggage—simply
the clothes I stand in

that place where poems
began for them, where
apocalypse occurred
in the ordinary.

I now go to prepare
an ordinary meal
but carry the fullness
of someone else's

raw intimacy
into the world of
parsnips, potatoes
cinnamon and salt.

IV

Thoughts for Your Penny   43

Thoughts for Your Penny

1

the cat comes
careful not to make friends
only contacts

2

all young tender things
come first green

3

caparisoned for the wedding
of summer to winter . . .
a white heron
white chrysanthemum
and a torrent of
hurricane-hurled
white water

4

fog is a gentler of
sharp edges
harsh colors
a smoother and softer . . .
a kindness

5

I thought it would be there
always
because I saw it once

I thought I could look
another day
and all would be the same

6

like huddled
        hibernating things
my frightened thoughts
        of you bed down
        in hollow dark
to keep each other warm

7

the first snow
mixed with the last of the
thistle-down
makes an unseasonably
fine flurry

8

only by touching
the hem of the past
can I be made whole

9

in my grandmother's
perverse mind
the thundering
surf-sound
is coal delivered
in a metal chute

10

my voice sings back to me
     across the lake

if my timing is right
     I could be in harmony
with myself

read to here

11

the seasons are only
circular to the old

when you are young
there is an endless string
of dew-fresh days

12

the moon's half

not large enough
to start a sudden romance
with anyone who

comes along
but bright enough
to light
remembered
tender things

13

when I am with you
I cannot sing

when I am away from you
it is you who
make me sing

14

my sundial says
it's not yet time to eat

my hunger says it is

my heart tells me
I should have
gone home long ago

15

where I live
spring comes
tight and guarded

it has millennial reasons
not to trust

its vulnerable green
to the first
blandishments of may

16

IF YOU LIVED HERE
says the sign
YOU'D BE HOME NOW

what is this future
toward which I strain
in senseless hurry?

17

in a sudden mirror
the startled sight of me
reflecting
the gray outside only
nothing of the child-colors
marbling the inside

18

"even today
at age of seventy-three
I remember
the ships' names
as if they were poems"
said the Japanese pilot
trained for the strike

arizona   utah   nevada...
sing the remembered names
for the remembered dead

19

the dry wind
drove sand
in the face of
our first try
at civilization
swept it
deep under
blasted its
memory
left us to
try again
somewhere else
some fertile
river-land
fair enough
to image a
new testament

V

√

Words   51

Toward Forever   53

The Rest of Her Life   54

Postprandial Snapshot   55

Loving Matters   56

Country Cousins   57

For My Sister, Now   59

New Born   60

Words

Words are such damn pesky things
heavy too and oddly shaped
like field rock out of which
you want to build a pasture wall.

They're not inanimate, you know,
those stones will quick as anything
turn sudden-like and crush your hand

and sometimes when you think
you'd have one steady if
you only chocked it here
or under there—

it lets you think it's solid,
will bear another one on top
and then slides off and rolls down
laughing in the grass.

It's downright frustrating to try
to build with these unhandy things.

I keep on trying though
because just once—
last Fall, I think it was—
I hefted up a stone, too heavy really,
should have used a sled

staggered over to my half-built wall
and heaved it up on top.
It struck and stuck there
firm and sure and right

propped on three perfect points
and looking curiously light
without the need of chocking-stones
or anything.

"That's good," I said,
"that's very good."
I can't forget how good that felt.

It felt as good as when
last May, I think it was—
I tried to say *I love you*
and I said it right

and you received it
firm and sure and right
without the need of
talking half the night.

"That's good," I said,
"that's very good."
I can't forget how good that felt.

Toward Forever

Somewhere in the middle of a mystery
marriage creates itself
out of scraps of whole cloth

singing its own song
different from any song yet known
but familiar and sweet
as if remembered,

words known since childhood
music invented, improvising
as it goes along

a tune hummed in the headlong heart
needing always the harmony
of companion counterpoint
to make of two private and particular pasts
one new and surprising future.

Somewhere in the middle of a mystery
marriage recreates itself—again—again
reaching beyond the gently curved
and distancing horizon toward forever.

The Rest of Her Life

for my sister

Lord, carry her
on this swift river
of loving
over the rough rocks
of grieving

till she finds footing
on the soft sands
of a quieter shore

where, dripping wet
from recent baptism
she may step out
on new ground
under the comfort
of an old sun

clothed in old memory
haloed in new spirit
shining with possibility.

Postprandial Snapshot

We never got to the pies
recumbent on the coffee table,
their contribution to the evening
being their pumpkin-spice,
fragrant cinnamon, nutmeg, clove,
and the mother-country-God
smell of autumn apples.

One of us slid down on the sofa
succumbing to the languor
of after-dinner lassitude.
One of us, still upright,
legs splayed out in front of him
seemed to be pondering
his next weighty pronouncement,

while I waited patiently
to interject my stunningly cogent
remark which seemed brilliant
at the time but, recalled the next day,
appeared somewhat wanting
in substance, logic, coherence,
perhaps even, oh damn, relevance.

Loving Matters

You ploughed and cultivated
the new ground of my body
planting lovingly, as I've seen you

patting the soil with
the flat of your hand
hoping to secure the seed

before a quick-eyed crow,
early drought, or spring downpour
carries off the promise.

All is chance—little to control.
Only the loving matters.

Country Cousins

"It's so quiet here!"
my cousin exclaims
over and over in
New York wonderment,

deaf to the churring
night-song of the cicadas,
the bullfrogs' attempt at *Tea for Two,*
red-eyed whip-poor-wills

insistent wolf whistle
and the tree frogs' swelling
and receding waves
of syncopated sound.

Under the near-full
moon the coy-dogs
howl in chorus
across the night fields.

Can she fail to hear
the snare-drum chatter
of thieving raccoons in
the just-ripe corn and

the soughing summer breeze
carrying the blunt
stomp of deer
under the apple tree?

Visiting her, I lie stiffly
alert to a nightmare
of loud images: piercing
whine of summoning sirens

whoop-whoop of cruisers
navigating night streets
crashing cymbal-sounds
of tossed garbage can lids

 and the disturbing dialogue
of a combative drunk with
a passive-aggressive lamp post—
while my cousin sleeps soundlessly.

For My Sister, Now

Now—while I can still
speak her living name
and turn back the precise pain
of sharp abandonment I so fear,

I shall write a poem—
for my sister—dead.

I must practice this darkness
as I practiced blindness when a child,
eyes squeezed shut

against the haunting time
of loss.

New Born

I went home
And turned on all the lights
Because I thought
That if I did she would be well
Death's darkness would recede

I did not want to be alone with death
Not while first breaths came
Through tubes and wires
No mother's arms or father's kiss
Not while sweet life lay
So fragile, tentative
As if she sensed
That death still claimed her
Not to pay a debt
Or right a wrong
Or to atone
But just for grief

I do not pray
Because I know
No one is listening
There is no shield against the dark
But I have cried all day
And I have lit
Every light I own
Although I know
She cannot see
Her newborn eyes are shut
And they have taken her

So far away
But maybe she will feel
Within her tiny heart
Against the hovering darkness
All my lights

VI

vi

Magic Man	65
Acceptance	67
Inconstant Moon	68
Oak Leaves	69
The Scent of Lilacs	70
Into the Silence	71
Whom Do I Thank?	72
Bethlehem in Judea	73
Why Not Angels?	75

9

64

Magic Man

The Magic Man
marks circles in the dust
as magic-making children always do,
dividing sacred from profane,
delineating space, mandala-like
for power to be manifest.

The circle is a magic thing—
the Druids knew.
It draws within its geometric self
as burning glass, the sun,
the fire from heaven—
or hell or any other place
the gods may dwell.

The children know
before they're ever told,
the ring-around-the-rosy things
that clearly show who's out—
who's in—and with the canniness
of young and weak, they seek
to manage their unmanageable world
with symbols.

I make my circles—
dare my gods to come
and thunder horribly
on my behalf. They laugh.

On my behalf they laugh
and slowly walk the circle round

tracing a clear mandala
on the ground.

The Magic Man
marks circles in the dust
but knows the roundness
doesn't mean the powers must
obey his least command.
His magic is an invitation,
to laugh.

Acceptance

A few fair-weather clouds
sail across the blue
of the summer sky
driven by the vigor
of a weather-changing wind.

The oaks dance, maples wave
and the white pine needles
shiver a brisk *obligato*.
Nothing is certain, they say,
but death and taxes.

Weather, however, is
a lesson in acceptance.
A rainy 4th of July taxes
the ingenuity and resilience
of the American spirit.

Where do all the prayers go
that are so desperately prayed for:
a fair day for an outdoor wedding,
a family reunion without a tent,
crops thirsty for a downpour?

Inconstant Moon

There's promise
of fullness
in the silver
sliver of moon
slung casually
in the frame of my
winter window.

I'm a little sorry
that I know
its shape is
constant and round.

There's wonderment
in the waxing,
and in the waning,
a needful resignation.

Oak Leaves

Spring is late this year
but the chill wind has torn
the crisp, brown oak leaves
from the twigs and branches
to which they've clung
the whole long Winter.

They scratch and stutter
across the wide sidewalk
making syncopated rhythms
of the most sophisticated
seductive sort, like the sound
of ten tiny snare drums,

sounds suitable for beguiling all
millipedes within hearing
into a wild stampede of joy
—but you must close your eyes
to behold this wonderment or you will
see only crisp brown oak leaves.

The Scent of Lilacs

The lilacs are in full bloom
and on the rapid transport
of their sweet scent
I am again four years old

living next door to Mrs. Smith
whose property line was marked
by a dense, fragrant hedge
of white and lavender blooms.

Mrs. Smith was bringing up
her grandson, just my age,
for reasons too grown-up for me
to be told, or even understand.

Most mornings her grandson
would crawl through the lilacs,
cross our narrow property to
go play with the plumber's son.

And each morning, if I was patient
he would return to play with me
after being beat-up by the
plumber's son's older brothers.

At four, one can learn *life lessons:*
the way things are, the way they work.
Patience is not just a virtue, it's useful—
as the scent of lilacs reminds me.

Into the Silence

If you sit quietly long enough
your spirit peaceful
chipmunks will find
nothing to fear
and will dart
by your quietness
playing about your feet
as though you were
a natural part
of their safe world.

If you sit quietly enough
the small peaceable thoughts
which have been relegated
to the far corners
of your daily mind
the sly thoughts
the unremembered things
will feel safe enough
to remind you
who you are
how you came to be so
and what seemingly irrelevant things
went into shaping
the person you've become.

Whom Do I Thank?

Whom do I thank
for the gladsome
yellow hibiscus
blooms blossoming
to my need,

for the August-gentle
breeze fanning
the solitary spot
where I sit to think,

for birdsong, blueberries,
the random patterns
of leaf shadows
spread on the path
for my pleasure?

Surely the God of this
infinity of universe
has more important
things to do than
take note of thanks
from a small bluish
planet circling a
not very large sun
in an insignificant galaxy.

Or are my imaginings
too limited —
is my God too small?

Bethlehem in Judea

It must have been a place
like any other place where
people go about their business

make a living
have their ups and downs
go to and fro
make bread, weave cloth
tend sheep, pay taxes,

tell lies and hurt each other,
love, and often miss
the point of loving—

an ordinary place
a not extraordinary time
except for one thing.

There were some,
open and expectant,
willing to listen to angels,

even on the hillside
where they went
to tend their sheep,

who were sore afraid
on that occasion
but not surprised
to encounter angels.

Why Not Angels?

Expecting harps, haloes, hymns—
and, of course, wings—
we look unseeing
at angels in aprons, saris, loincloths,
dressed as moving men,
taxi drivers, passersby,

angels with soft jazzy voices,
angels with wispy white hair
blue dresses and anxious faces,
angels with barked shins,
scraped knees and untied shoelaces

whose ministrations,
attentions, graces,
are recognized only later
if at all,
by words like
coincidence,
happenstance,
fate

but for those attuned
to astonishments,
alive to surprise,

the word is
angels
and the response is
wonderment.

Carol Armstrong has written poetry most of her life, as did her mother before her, at odd hours of the day on the back of envelopes or grocery lists. She has written from childhood through college and continued through the years of raising three children and sharing the career of her husband, James Armstrong, at Middlebury College.

In her 96th year, she continues to participate in poetry groups regularly. This volume is the second collection of her poems following *Everything Waits to be Noticed* (Antrim House 2011).

She lives in Hanover New Hampshire.